Real Christmas Poetry

Steve Page

What?

Each Christmas brings new poetry – here's Steve's poetry from 2019-2022.

Who?

Steve lives in Ealing and worships at Redeemer London each Sunday at the University of West London.   And each Christmas he writes fresh Christmas poetry, some of which finds its way to the Christmas Carol Concert.

Why?

Good question.   Hopefully to stir a heart and raise a smile.

Why now?

In 2018 Steve collected his yuletide poetry in 'Not too soon for Christmas'.   Here's the next instalment.

Introduction

I love Christmas.

That's it.

Simple as that.

It's one of the best parts of being a Christian. And while I sometimes find I can create a tension – you know, between all the glitter and all the real stuff – mostly I find a balance between the two.

That's sometimes reflected in my poetry. Some reflect my faith, some reflect my sense of fun.

I hope both seep through the pages and give you some pause for thought and pleasure.

Merry Christmas.

Luke 1

The first Christmas started with:

"Do not be afraid, Mary;

you have found favour with God…"

There's another tension right there: fear and favour.

You chose.

Christmas Mash

November 2019

May your bells jingle all the way

      May your snow be crisp and even

May your ding dong merrily on high

      And may Saint Nick keep you believing

Advent 2019

November 2019

I hold with care the value of the Wait

with a backdrop of the intrusion of the Immediate;

I relish the Not Yet,

not looking for an untimely rush into the Unfinished;

I anticipate the delicious Hope,

ignoring the clamour of dissent;

and not taking anything for granted,

I do all I can to clear space,

to listen with intent

and to then herald the Promise of the Soon,

the ready-coming-King,

and I embrace the God-With-Us.

Now.

The Christmas preposition is 'with'.

God <u>with</u> us.

Rudolph The Red

November 2019

Rudolph The Red stayed in his shed
Unhappy with minimum wage
He refused to get started
Cos he wasn't rewarded
With the promised end of year raise

Rudolph The Red sang with his friends
And staged an all-advent sit-in
But Santa just smiled
Cos his jet had been fuelled
In advance for such an occasion

Rudolph The Red looked overhead
While Santa sped round the world
When Santa got back
With his large empty sack
His workshop was empty of Elves

Rudolph The Red was no longer led
By thoughts of personal gain
He'd formed his first union
With Elves and ten Snowmen
And the workers were free once again

There's a giant red reindeer in Ealing square.

It started me thinking.

The thrill of Hope

November 2020

The thrill of **hope**

A **hope** of promise

Behold the **birth**

Of **joy** and solace

The birth of **love**

A **love** for life

Behold a **child**

A **born** delight

It seems we each need new Hope right now.

The thrill of Hope – extended version

December 2020

A weary world, a muted cry
uncertain plans and pleas denied

> But then a star, unearthly bright
> a glimpse of dawn, a new-found light

The thrill of hope, a hope of promise
Behold the birth of joy and solace

> The birth of love, the gift of life
> Behold a child, a born delight

The world in need calls out once more
prayers for relief, pleas for a cure

> And then He comes, the world rejoices
> Emmanuel, we raise our voices

His people stand, as one we sing
to our Messiah, our Saviour King

Advent 2020

December 2020

May you fare well during this Advent

May you find much grace as you wait

As your household houses his glory

And friends are well met at your gate

It's been quite a year. We spent a lot of time keeping to our households and keeping our distance.

Christmas 2021

December 2021

I noticed the sudden silence

balanced on the offbeat of a carol left incomplete,

but after a while I found - despite my long belief –

I was enjoying the competing peace

a little more than the jingle,

the insistent hush more than the chimes

the spreading rest more than the dance.

And I put it all down

to the close-knit company.

A quieter Christmas with my son and his dear wife.

Come now

December 2021

God said, come now

and let us mystery together,

fire and phoenix together,

rhythm together, step together,

be danced and held together.

Let us rest in my meadow,

feast to our pleasure

and pour to our brim-full altogether.

Come let us be here together.

A rift off Isaiah 1:18

Greatest Gift

December 2021

They say that it's the thought that counts ...
and I wonder how He counted the cost,
from the first conception of His salvation plan
to the final arrival of God made man.

What were His first infant thoughts?
What did He think of His mother's first touch?
And the assault of the cold, the earthy smells?
And perhaps the chime of several cow bells?

Each chime heralding this greater gift,
out-giving even a mother's first kiss,
or the gifts from shepherds and eastern kings.
This God-gift out-gave all they could bring.

They say that it's the thought that counts
and I count this gift of Immanuel,
this Godly-conceived first Noel
as by far the Greatest Gift of all.

Written for RedeemerLondon.org preparing for Christmas 2021

Greatest Gift 2

December 2021

So...
once the wrapping's been wrapped
and the gifts have been given
once bells have been rung
as is our tradition

once the turkey's a carcass
while mince pies remain
(and you wonder if salt
will lift that wine stain)

that's the time to receive
the one Gift worth having
the Christ of this Christmas
the Gift come from heaven

the Gift that's the Greatest
the Gift that kept giving
the Christ who stayed with us
the joy that kept coming

So ...
as the carols' words fade
don't let this chance drift
welcome Christ this Christmas
the Greatest Gift

Written for RedeemerLondon.org preparing for Christmas.

Reluctant leaf

September 2022 (yeah okay, it's not quite Christmas)

I'd make a lousy leaf …

I couldn't happily leave my tree, my family, my home

I expect I'd be one of the last, holding on, looking down

and nervously watching my siblings.

Seeing them heaped and occasionally lifted

to fly, to dance in a whirl of excitement

– free of past commitments.

Maybe then I'd gather my brittle courage,

eyes clenched shut, ready at last to jump

and to let go, into the unknown.

Only to find myself kicked around by ignorant children

who have no appreciation

of the journey I've been on to get here.

Oh well, this is a new season.

There's no going back now.

Carols collated (spot the Carol)

From my back catalogue.

These three kings of orient are
unfairly competing with one little drummer boy,
all dashing through the snow for the last boughs of holly
to lay them before the King.

Meanwhile three ships come sailing in
and certain poor shepherds leave their hot chestnuts,
each keen to hail the heaven-born Prince of Peace.

Later,
in Royal David's city,
there are ladies leaping, pipers piping
and drummers ...
drumming, apparently.
The restless cattle are lowing big-time;
no wonder the baby's awake.

All have come to proclaim the Messiah's birth;
this king-of-angels baby
who out-shines any wondrous star.
A child born of Mary, on this most holy of nights;
born to give us second birth:
This is the Saviour who is Christ the Lord,
come to redeem us all.

'Come – receive – your - king.'

Merry Christmas.

A mash up of some old carols – still heavy with meaning.

Also from Steve Page

If you enjoyed this collection, you just might enjoy

Not Too Big To Weep;

Not Too Old To Dance;

Not Too Soon For Christmas;

Father is a Verb;

Fruity Poetry; and

Wisdom Poetry.

If you still want more, you can find me amongst a world-wide crowd of poets on https://hellopoetry.com

And if you're into prose try:

Deborah's Daughter; and

A man walks into a bar.

Printed in Great Britain
by Amazon